Written by
Jennifer Jackson Linck

Illustrated by
J. Caffee Cruz

Designed by
Markus Linde

Jennifer Jackson Linck

www.jenniferjacksonlinck.com

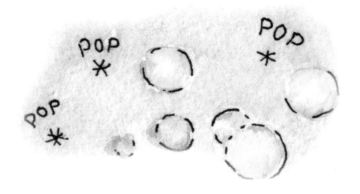

To Jackson
Your perseverance and courage inspire me!
Never forget that you are *fearfully and wonderfully made.*

To Jackson's Speech Therapists
Thank you for helping him find his voice.

"Before a word is on my tongue you,
Lord, know it completely…
For you created my inmost being;
you knit me together in my mother's womb.
I praise you because I am fearfully
and wonderfully made; your works are
wonderful, I know that full well."

Psalm 139: 4; 13-14

My name is Jackson. I'm on a journey to learn
new words and to one day sing my ABCs.

When I was a baby I didn't babble or coo,
But I wiggled and giggled Like other babies do.

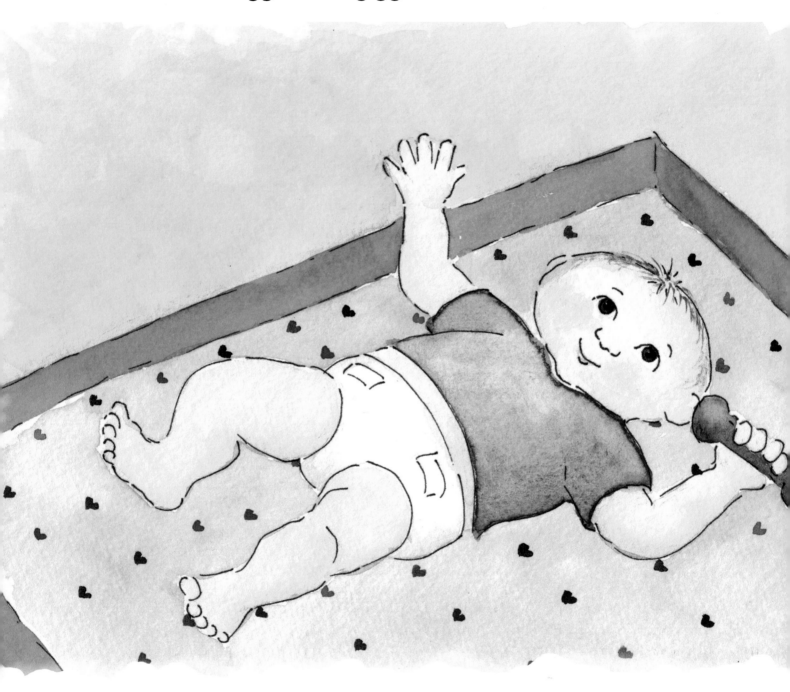

I said my first word when I was just one.
But *Mama* was all I said for such a long time.
When I turned two, I said a little more;
NO! quickly became my word of choice.

Then one day I started to bite. My mom knew something just wasn't right.
I would hit and pinch and get upset. So many words I just couldn't say yet.

So I started speech therapy.
Ms. Sarah made it fun.
Speech therapists help kids like me
learn words one by one.

We played with cars and trucks and trains; which are my favorite things.
We blew bubbles and practiced sounds
My *beeps* came out *deets*
But Mom said it was the cutest truck sound around.

I can't always call something by name,
but I can always tell you what things say.
I make the best fire truck and train sounds.
Woo Woo Woo.
Choo Choo Choo.

When I turned three, Ms. Sarah said I had Apraxia.
It was a big and scary word.
I know what I want to say, but simply can't.
The words get stuck in my brain,
My mouth hasn't caught up just yet.

With a lot of practice and a lot of love, I have learned many new words. Sometimes they sound funny, but I'm on my way to finding my voice.

Each new word was a cause for celebration!
Like the time I said Dr Pepper or the first time I said my name.

My parents went a little crazy!
They whooped and hollered and gave me high-fives.
Sometimes Mom even cried.
(She said it's because I inspired her)

I'm still three, and I'm saying more each day.
I can even say Dusty, the name of my favorite plane.

Most of my three-year-old friends can say more than me,
but that's okay. Mom says I'm
fearfully and wonderfully made.

Even though my words are few, I can still communicate with you.
Sometimes I use sign language.
But hugs and kisses and high-fives work, too!

Sometimes having a speech disorder isn't any fun.
I still get really mad when I can't say what's on my mind.
I'm different from other kids; but that's okay.
God says I'm *fearfully and wonderfully made.*

Mom says God has a special plan for me.
But sometimes His plans aren't always easy.
If I'll trust Him, come what may
He'll use my story to help others along the way.

God has a special plan for me; I believe it's true.
And I believe He has a special plan for YOU, too!

"For I know the plans I have for you," declares the Lord.
"Plans to prosper you and not to harm you.
Plans to give you hope and a future."

Jeremiah 29:11

What Is Childhood Apraxia of Speech?

Childhood apraxia of speech (CAS) is a motor
speech disorder. Children with CAS
have problems saying sounds, syllables, and words.
This is not because of muscle
weakness or paralysis. The brain has
problems planning to move the body parts
(e.g., lips, jaw, tongue) needed for speech.
The child knows what he or she wants to
say, but his/her brain has difficulty coordinating
the muscle movements necessary to say those words.
- American Speech-Language-Hearing Association

A child with Apraxia has to hear a word approximately
3,000 times before it becomes
a regular part of their vocabulary.
For more information about Childhood Apraxia of
Speech, visit http://www.apraxia-kids.org

Jennifer Jackson Linck has always wanted to write a children's book. When her son was diagnosed with Childhood Apraxia of Speech at age three, she was inspired to write about a little boy on a journey to find his voice.

Jackson Finds His Voice is Jennifer's first children's book. It was written as a tool to help her son tell his story, while raising awareness for Childhood Apraxia of Speech. Jennifer's previous books include *Bringing Home the Missing Linck: A Journey of Faith to Family and Trucks, Tantrums, & Trusting Him: Confessions of a Boy Mom.* She writes about faith and motherhood on her blog www.jenniferjacksonlinck.com. She lives in Oklahoma with her husband, John, and their son Jackson.

Made in the USA
Middletown, DE
08 November 2018